Four Concertos for Organ

£14·50

Four Concertos for Organ

George Frideric Handel

arranged by Colin Hand

We hope you enjoy the music in this book.
Further copies of this and our many other books are available
from your local music shop or Christian bookshop.

In case of difficulty, please contact the publisher direct by writing to:

The Sales Department
KEVIN MAYHEW LTD
Buxhall
Stowmarket
Suffolk IP14 3BW

Phone 01449 737978
Fax 01449 737834

Please ask for our complete catalogue of outstanding Church Music.

Front Cover: *Ecstasy of Saint Theresa,* sculpture by Giovanni Lorenzo Bernini (1598-1680).
Courtesy of Santa Maria della Vittoria, Rome / The Bridgeman Art Library, London.
Reproduced by kind permission.

Cover designed by Jaquetta Sergeant.

First published in Great Britain in 1997 by Kevin Mayhew Ltd.

© Copyright 1997 Kevin Mayhew Ltd.

ISBN 0 86209 957 9
ISMN M 57004 028 5
Catalogue No: 1400117

0 1 2 3 4 5 6 7 8 9

Music Editor: Donald Thomson
Music setting by Daniel Kelly

Printed and bound in Great Britain

Contents

CONCERTO IN B♭ MAJOR Op. 4 No. 2

George Frideric Handel (1685-1759) arr. Colin Hand

9

11

13

Sw. *mf*

Gt.

Sw.*mf*

cresc.

Gt.
8' 4' f

16' 8'

mf

Sw. (Ch.)
8' 4' 2'

tr

CONCERTO IN F MAJOR Op. 4 No. 5

George Frideric Handel (1685-1759) arr. Colin Hand

last time rall.

Gt.

Tempo di Siciliana

Solo 8'

Gt. 8' *mf*

Sw. 8'

29

30

CONCERTO IN D MINOR Op. 7 No. 4

George Frideric Handel (1685-1759) arr. Colin Hand

Attacca

38

39

41

Allegretto

45

46

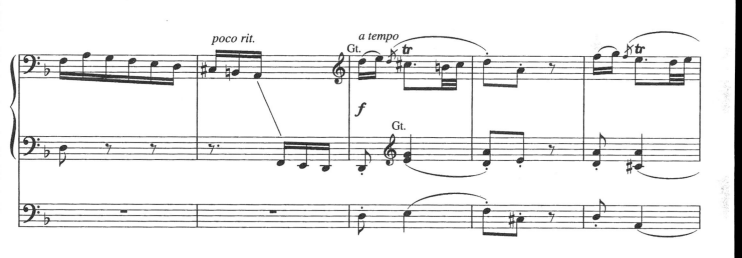

CONCERTO IN G MINOR Op. 7 No. 5

George Frideric Handel (1685-1759) arr. Colin Hand

Attacca

55

57

58

59